GOODNESS GRACE US

UNDERSTANDING GRACE THROUGH THE STORIES OF THE GRACELESS

ESSENCE PATTERSON

Goodness Grace Us

Copyright © 2019 Essence Patterson

ISBN: 9781078479608

All rights reserved.

This book or any portion thereof may not be reproduced or used in any manner whatsoever without the express written permission of the author, except for the use of brief quotations in a book review to be cited.

we do have stories of how God's grace kept us to share, we'd probably be remiss to keep them to ourselves, don't you think?

why it is crucial that my generation began to embrace and share their testimonies too.

As I was talking to one of my best friends about writing this book, I began to share with her a frustrating moment two of my other friends experienced during a recent gathering at the time. During this meeting, my two friends were jokingly told by someone that they were "born saved." Though it was known that it was a joke, it was still reciprocated with the shaky laughter that comes with awkward moments. It's statements like this, whether intended for good or bad, that create the assumption that those raised in church didn't have to "go through" anything in order to know God before giving their lives to Him; a scenario I related to greatly. It should also be noted that both of these friends of mine are Pastors' kids. As I discussed this while my friend drove, I felt my frustration spill over into a pile of words, questioning why people are the way they are and say what they say, especially church members. It wasn't until later that I'd realized the very frustration I felt transformed into the fuel I needed to want to write about encounters like this one, and hear even more stories, specifically from my generation, about striving to be the example 1 Timothy 4:12 discusses when the odds seem to be against us. Since the Word of God tells us to be angry but sin not, I realized that choosing to stay frustrated would lead to anger, and choosing to stay angry would ultimately lead me to sin. Therefore, my best bet (and the encouragement I should've given to my friends at the time) would be to hold onto the encounters I've had with God for myself, the challenges I've overcome with His help, and the restoration of love and grace I've felt each and every time, no matter what age I was, am, or will be; for without His grace, there would be no testimony, there'd be no me, there'd be no you. So, since we do have access to the gift of grace, and since understand, as I got older, that even if I couldn't pinpoint what I thought at that time was my testimony, I knew one thing remained the same: Jesus. He was the constant in my life, and continues to be my constant. It is in Him that I grew to understand that my testimony isn't just a one-time thing. It's the challenges I overcome through His Word each season I step into. It isn't just the experiences you had before you came to know Christ, it's that car accident you were in, but walked away from 10 years into being a believer. It's that eviction notice that was removed from your door 2 years after you were baptized. It's that family member you finally saw accept Jesus after praying for them for over 60 years. It's the stories we carry to testify to the goodness of God, whether they happen before we knew God or because we know God. I realized, though, that the determining factor I created for myself in understanding whether or not I had a "valid" testimony came down to one thing – my age.

Testimony service was something I became familiar with at a very young age, considering my roots are in the church. But the common denominator I observed of these said services were the ages of the people getting up to testify. Usually, it was a mother in the church, 60-80 years old, sharing a story of how God provided "a way out of no way" that would end in an impromptu selection of "How I Got Over." It wasn't until I got to college that I began seeing people of my age share what God had done in their lives. In fact, people would come up to me and ask, "what's your story?" and I would have no clue what they'd be referring to, but as they began opening up to me, sharing the details of how they got where they needed to be and the journeys God took them through to be positioned in the right place, I began to understand not only what a testimony is, but

Kingdom of God (don't let anyone tell you God can't do great things with small packages, but that's a different story to tell). At the age of four, many are learning to write their names, count to 100, and share. I, however, was different. Yes, I was learning those things, but I was also learning about who God was, why He sent His Son, and why this man named Jesus would choose to die for me, my parents, and the whole entire world. Some could argue and say that it was my parents' decision forced upon me or that I didn't really know what I was doing when I walked to the altar, but I'd be quick to remind you that the God I serve prioritizes children and their understanding of who He is, so there were definitely no mistakes or misunderstandings made in the process of my salvation. However, in full transparency of this book and its mission, I will gladly share that as I grew up, the concept of having my own testimony was foreign to me, due to the very fact that I was only four when I gave my life to Christ.

I believe it was a summer at church camp (there was always a proper name for it, but my friends and I just went with "church camp") where the topic of testimonies came up. Hearing how the Lord works in each and every one of our lives in a customized fashion, tailor-made to fit our very own relationship with Him was such an encouraging message to embrace. I, however, began to panic when I was introduced to the meaning of a testimony. I guess it was the way that it was presented to me that threw me off. "What you were doing..." and "who you were before you came to know Christ..." I realized were two phrases I couldn't connect to, unless, of course, if they were speaking in a literal sense. That would be that I was watching Sesame Street, singing Silly Songs with Larry, and eating oatmeal any chance I got. What did that have to do with me finding out who Jesus is? I panicked. But what I grew to

PREFACE

I remember being at work one morning, seeing one of my four-year-old students come in one of the happiest moods I'd ever seen her in. She was twirling around in the hallways while simultaneously grasping her mother's phone which was blasting "Testimony" by Anthony Brown & Group TherAPY. As I walked by with a light chuckle and a beaming smirk on my face, I overheard her mother explaining to someone in the hallway how her daughter instantly connected with the song and that she couldn't understand why she loved it so much. Now granted, maybe it was because of the melodious, upbeat tempo of the song itself, but who's to say she didn't connect with the words? In fact, this scenario that literally took less than one minute for me to experience made me reminisce all the way back to myself at that age. You see, at the age of four, I became a believer; I gave my life to Christ in the basement of a building located in downtown Ramstein-Miesenbach, Germany. That basement was known as Agape Christian Faith Centre, and would later make its home from a basement to a local storefront, where despite its location, created a global impact for The

TABLE OF CONTENTS

PREFACE vii

PART ONE: THE CONCEPT OF GRACE 1

CHAPTER 1: Defining Grace 3

CHAPTER 2: Grace & Mercy: The Power Couple 7

CHAPTER 3: Why Is It So Amazing? 9

CHAPTER 4: Your Testimony Isn't Just For You 17

CHAPTER 5: The Testimony Equation 21

PART TWO: ACKNOWLEDING THE GRACELESS 25

CHAPTER 6: Who Are "The Graceless?" 27

PART THREE: MY FIRST DATE WITH GRACE 41

CHAPTER 7: The Gracious Rendezvous 43

PART FOUR: THE STRUGGLE IS REAL, BUT SO ARE WE ... 49

CHAPTER 8: Use Your Voice 51

CHAPTER 9: Wrapped A Little Differently 59

CHAPTER 10: Be The Demo 63

PART FIVE: IF HIS GRACE IS LIKE AN OCEAN, ARE WE SWIMMING? 69

CHAPTER 11: Texas And Tubin' 71

CHAPTER 12: Floating. Sinking. Swimming 75

ACKNOWLEDGEMENTS 83

ABOUT THE AUTHOR 88

Grace. 5 letters that changed the whole trajectory of Christianity.

5 letters that can change the hope of our generation.

To The Graceless, may you forever seek The One Who holds your purpose in His hand.

This is for you.

PART ONE

THE CONCEPT OF GRACE

CHAPTER 1

DEFINING GRACE

Let me first start by saying this: I am not one to pretend to know what I'm talking about, when I have absolutely no clue. I'm at a point in life now where I realize the value of transparency and vulnerability like never before. With that being said, though I am more than confident in knowing that I've seen, received and experienced God's grace over and over – countless times – I am still learning what this concept of grace is too. To me, it's like the equivalent of someone saying that math is their favorite subject, which would not be me (By the way, this will *not* be the only time I talk about this. I mention my dispassion for math several times, so do me a favor and tally up just how many times I mention math and DM me on Instagram with the answer… Seriously.). Despite having yet to solve every mathematical equation or even be introduced to every theory, you've grown an understanding of it and have a great appreciation for it. I believe it was my favorite songwriter, Jonathan McReynolds, that helped me understand it best. He said that basically, God is showing him everything he's meant to share with others while he's still experiencing what that is, so instead of speaking to people from a place of having mastered it all, God's simply using him to speak from a place of constant learning. My prayer is that you may still receive what the Lord has given to me to share concerning His grace in your life as I continue to receive what He desires to share with me concerning His grace in mine.

When Googled (because let's be honest, we probably haven't sought out a physical dictionary in months, if not years), the word "grace" is given several definitions. Here are a few:

1. simple elegance or refinement of movement
2. courteous goodwill
3. a short prayer of thanks said before or after a meal
4. do honor or credit to (someone or something) by one's presence

And the one that stuck out to me the most:

5. (in Christian belief) the free and unmerited favor of God, as manifested in the salvation of sinners and the bestowal of blessings
   - a divinely given talent or blessing
   - the condition or fact of being favored by someone

It has been clearly set before us that the grace God grants us is one, attained through salvation, but two, FREE and not deserved. Meaning there is nothing we've done to earn it and nothing we can do to earn it. Salvation, believing Jesus was sent to this earth by God, to take on the sin of the world and die on a cross at Calvary where He would be taken off, put in a tomb, but rise three days later with all power in His hand, gives us the key to experience God's grace. However, God's grace, just like the word itself, has varying forms. Grace to one may look like finding your lost shoe after asking for guidance from The Holy

Spirit, thinking you'd be late to work, while grace to another may look like walking away from a car accident without a scratch. Grace is grace.

Let's put it into a different perspective. Lying is a pretty point-blank-period concept to understand, and it's usually deemed awful in the eyes of most. Yet some believe in something called a "white lie;" a lie seen on a lower scale of impact to justify the intention of the lie itself. But in the end, we all know a lie is a lie, whether you label it white, black, purple or red. It's the same with grace, the favor of God. There is no such thing as a "white grace" because with grace, there is nothing to justify. There is nothing miniscule about the impact of grace in one's life, no matter how it is encountered. This book is here to be an encouragement to others that the gift of grace is a free one; one you can rely and depend on each and every day, and one that reminds you of who God is no matter how many times the world may try to remind you of who you used to be. 2 Corinthians 5:17 (CEV) says, "Anyone who belongs to Christ is a new person. The past is forgotten, and everything is new." Everything is new, including God's grace for you each morning and here's the proof! In Lamentations 3 (CEV), the prophet is sharing how he first viewed God as someone who wanted nothing but trouble for him. He states how his own thoughts almost caused him to turn his back on God, but then his tone changes in verse 21 where he says, "Then I remember something that fills me with hope." He then continues in verse 22 saying, "The Lord's kindness never fails! If he had not been merciful, we would have been destroyed." Right after, he makes this bold proclamation for us as believers to hold onto, "The Lord can always be trusted to show mercy each morning." "Well Essence, He said 'mercy' not 'grace.'" I'm glad you picked up on that. I introduce to you, grace and mercy, The Power Couple.

CHAPTER 2

GRACE & MERCY: THE POWER COUPLE

Looking at grace and mercy, love and kindness, glory and honor, and other sanctified, "churchy" if you will, pairings mentioned in Christianity, it's no coincidence that they are often coupled together like this. This, I believe, is because without one, you can't truly experience the other, and when put together, you get the ultimate emphasis and power of both words and their role in Christian living. For example, love and kindness are usually intertwined in Christian vocabulary (sometimes the word "compassion" may take the place of "kindness," but the meaning is still the same). Love, we know, is both a feeling and an action. In this case, kindness, being the ability to show and act in concern and empathy toward someone or something, is the action result of love, while kindness can also provoke the feeling of love. In layman's terms, I'm kind because I love you, and because you've been kind to me, I feel loved. It's the same with grace and mercy. We've already laid out the many definitions of grace, but here's the definition of mercy (again, thanks Google):

1. compassion or forgiveness shown toward someone whom it is within one's power to punish or harm.
    - an event to be grateful for, especially because its occurrence prevents something unpleasant or provides relief from suffering.
    - (especially of a journey or mission) performed out of a desire to relieve suffering; motivated by compassion.

Mercy extends the essence of grace. It is because of God's mercy we are able to experience His grace. Just as kindness is a direct result of love, grace is a direct result of mercy. God, being all-powerful, all-knowing, worthy of all glory, and ever-present is more than capable of using His power to belittle, cut down, and deem us powerless in ways that we'd have no way to pull ourselves back together, but He chooses not to. His love and mercy are so sufficient that His grace was a non-negotiable part of the contract Jesus agreed to and that we get to benefit from through salvation. He decided that despite the short-comings He knew we'd have, despite not praying enough, despite not reading our Bibles enough and choosing to scroll through Instagram and down Facebook first thing in the morning instead, despite not listening to the unction of His Holy Spirit, a gift He has yet again graced us with, despite being prideful in our ever so human naturistic ways, He still chose grace through mercy. We're constantly blessed and favored daily by our almighty God because of His mercy shown toward us daily. Thank you, God.

CHAPTER 3

WHY IS IT SO AMAZING?

If that last section wasn't enough to answer this question, let's do a little more digging. If you don't know already, I'm kind of a nerd. English was my favorite subject in school and researching is a spare-time hobby of mine, so I figured, "Why not put two together and create the opportunity for one of my favorite words to come to life – analysis?" Whether it be due to a church service, a funeral, or even watching a film, "Amazing Grace" is a recognizable melody to millions across the world. Me being the self-proclaimed researcher that I am, I decided the best way to further enhance our understanding of grace and its' role is to take a look at these lyrics:

Amazing Grace by John Newton

> *Amazing Grace! How sweet the sound*
> *That saved a wretch like me.*

I once was lost, but now am found,
Was blind but now I see
T'was grace that taught my heart to fear,
And grace, my fears relieved.
How precious did that grace appear
The hour I first believed.

Through many dangers, toils and snares
I have already come;
'Tis grace that brought me safe thus far
And grace will lead me home,
And grace will lead me home

Okay, so let's break it down:

Amazing Grace! How sweet the sound
That saved a wretch like me.
I once was lost, but now am found,
Was blind but now I see

This, I believe, is the most popular stanza. In it, the writer describes grace not only as amazing, but as a sound that is sweet to the ears. He then goes on to say that this sweet-sounding, amazing grace saved him, despite him being a wretch. Now I'm not going to front, I had to go look up the word "wretch." I knew I'd heard it before in the scripture where Paul cries out "O wretched man that I am! Who will deliver me from this body of death?" (Romans 7:24 NLT) But that still didn't give me the clear definition I was looking for. According to Dictionary.com, wretch as a noun is defined as "a deplorably unfortunate or unhappy person." It is then also defined as "a person of despicable or base character." So as a wretch, not only are you as a person unhappy, but your character is lacking as well. The stanza proceeds in stating, "I once was lost, but now I'm found. Was blind, but now I see." Based off the definition of wretch alone, it is clear that living a lifestyle of a wretch correlates to being far from a place of clarity and understanding. Thus, feeling lost in your purpose and feeling blinded from all the hope and potential life offered in Christ. Thank God for His grace, powerful enough to rescue and deliver us from lifestyles of unhappiness, harmful mentalities, and beliefs of purposelessness!

> *T'was grace that taught my heart to fear,*
> *And grace, my fears relieved.*
> *How precious did that grace appear*
> *The hour I first believed.*

The first thing that sticks out to me in this verse is the word "fear." In the first line, the writer is crediting grace for teaching him how to fear. Now you might be thinking, "Well, that doesn't make sense," when in fact, it makes perfect sense and here's why. The fear this line refers to is that of reverence; beholding something in such a valuable manner and giving it the respect, honor, and attention, it deserves. We then see that in the next line, grace was also the reason the songwriter's fears, the definition we're most familiar with, were relieved. Ultimately, grace not only shows you the importance of reverencing God and putting your heart before Him, but it is also the reason why you can overcome any and everything that is not like Him that may be trying to keep you from living the life He's destined you to.

> *Through many dangers, toils and snares*
> *I have already come;*

> *'Tis grace that brought me safe thus far*
> *And grace will lead me home,*
> *And grace will lead me home*

I'm a very big Disney fan and one of my favorite movies to watch when I was younger was *The Incredibles* (and I still love it despite them taking nearly 15 years to come out with the sequel). In the movie, a family of superheroes is learning how to navigate their superpowers in the real world after all superheroes and heroines have been banned from using their powers, especially in public. However, because a villain has taken the father, Mr. Incredible, into his custody, the kids, Dash, Violet, and Jack-Jack, along with their mother, ElastiGirl, have no choice but to use their powers in an effort to find and rescue him. In one of the most action-packed scenes, the family (sans Jack-Jack) finds themselves being chased throughout the jungle by the army of the villain they're after. In the jungle, we get to see each of their encounters that showcase their superpowers, specifically Dash's speed and Violet's forcefield invisibility. Though each of them are being targeted, they ultimately end up in the same area after Dash rescues his sister from being shot. However, the shooter then turns the gun on Dash, but Violet, in an attempt to save Dash, jumps and releases a protective shield whilst in midair. Dash than proceeds to ask, "How are you doing that?" to which Violet answers, "I don't know." After telling his sister to continue doing whatever it is she's doing, he begins to take off. With this combination of their powers, they are able to create a protected a form of transportation to navigate through the jungle. Whew! Now that my in-depth commentary has ended, back to where we were. That scene is what this verse reminds me of. The first and second line state "through many dangers, toils and snares I have already come," meaning that regardless of whatever trouble the songwriter faced, he lived to tell the story and share his testimony because of what the next line discusses; grace leading to a safe place. Like Dash and Violet's makeshift protective shield through the jungle, I thoroughly believe grace is similar in likeness. It is with God's grace that not only are we protected, but we are also directed.

As a teacher, I understand the importance of simplicity and providing explanations in layman's terms. That being said, if you don't get anything else, here's the thing about grace: it's not something that can be achieved or rewarded at the end of a finish line. Grace is accessible in every area of your life whether you be four, seven, twenty-five, or ninety-two living in Europe, Asia, or The United States. But it is *not* to be taken for granted. The gift of grace is something to help continue to ignite our faith in Christ, The One, True and Living God. But when we decide to use this gift as a "get out of jail free card," as one of my friends so eloquently puts it, we ignore the thing that caused grace to exist in the first place – love. Choosing to purposely do the things we've been commanded as believers *not* to do simply because "well, there's grace," in my eyes, is the equivalent of slapping God in the face. Here, our Heavenly Father is gracing us with His goodness and mercy because He is so loving and caring toward us, and instead of choosing to glorify him with our lives, we choose to be selfish and pick the things that temporarily satisfy us, knowing that God is a forgiving God. However, what many fail to grasp is that forgiveness can only take place when true reflection is present. The confession in knowing that you've done wrong and that God is the only One Who can cleanse you, deliver you and set you free, through the power of His Son Jesus is what causes grace to overwhelm us in the greatest of ways. But when we walk around, prideful in our wrong doings, fully aware of the things that keep us from having our deepest relationship with God, we're choosing to make a mockery out of who God says He is and all that He has done for us. Make no mistake; I'm talking to myself too. The conviction is strong with this one. The time has run out for excuses to keep our egos boosted and our pride in play. No more "God knows my heart"s and "only God can judge me"s as justifications because I assure you, both of these things are true, but not in the way you'd like them to be. It is true He does know your heart and He is judging you. So ask yourself if He is pleased when He looks at who you are and what you are doing in and with your life. Is what you're doing bringing Him glory, or only bringing you pleasure? Is it encouraging and uplifting others, or causing bitterness toward people in your heart? Think about it like this: if you were given the most precious of gifts for your birthday, anniversary, Christmas, etc. and it was something that when you opened, it instantly gave you immense joy and happiness, you wouldn't ruin and destroy it just because the person who gave it to you may possibly get you another one, would you? In fact, chances are they'd probably never gift you with anything again. Now, let's switch perspectives. What if you were the gift-giver? How would you feel, knowing that the thought and meaning you placed into selecting this gift for this person, the value it offered and the joy it would bring, has now been ruined due to the gift purposely being mishandled and destroyed by the one you gave it to? And now it's expected of you to give yet another gift! We would probably flip! But that's how I picture our Heavenly Father feeling when we choose to justify and excuse our actions for the advantage of his gift of grace. But thank God He is not one to hold back from us. He continues to shower us with his love and mercy day-after-day, mess-up-after-mess-up, He chooses to love us. *"For God saved us and called us to live a holy life. He did this, not because we deserved it, but because that was His plan from before the beginning of time – to show us his grace through Christ Jesus."* 2 Timothy 1:9 (NLT) In other words, God chose to love us, and keep loving us, from the very start, wanting what was best for us. At the very least, we owe Him our love too.

CHAPTER 4

YOUR TESTIMONY ISN'T JUST FOR YOU

While writing this book, the Lord gave me an equation to help remember why sharing our testimonies, our stories of grace, with others is so important. You see, we tend to think selfishly when it comes to sharing our testimony, not purposely, but it happens! We become so concerned about what others may say about us or how they would perceive us after sharing, when the truth is sharing our story could be the very thing that activates someone else's breakthrough. We can get so wrapped up in whether or not we feel comfortable sharing what, first of all, only God has brought us through, not ourselves, and how through God's grace we overcame, not realizing that souls are on the line. While we're sitting here going back and forth as to whether or not we should share what has happened in our past or what may be happening even now, God is looking at the bigger picture watching us, thinking "If only you would trust Me." We may think we are able to see what's in front of us, and we may think we know how to get to the next step. But I like to think of God's vision as the equivalent of the zoom button on a camera; not only can He zoom in on us to see what issues are going on in our lives and what our heart's posture is toward them, but He can also zoom all the way out and see just how many people we're connected to, how many events in life are awaiting us, and ultimately, how our response to His promptings affects each and every one of these things. "But Essence, you don't understand. I've gone through some pretty bad things and I've done even more messed up things." That may very well be true, and I'm not one to knock the heaviness of anything because we each hold a different weight limit. But what I do know is that you do not have to worry about those things, nor carry those burdens in your life anymore because it is those very things that will hold you back from truly experiencing the joy and splendor of God's grace. I recently heard someone say, "There is nothing too ugly for God," and it just gave me such an urge to want to grab a megaphone and shout it to everyone I know! Your past may have been ugly, the epitome of a hot mess, but guess what? God knows and He cares. Your flaws may have caused you to sink to a really hard place in your life, but guess what? God still loves you – always has, always will. So how about we stop carrying the heaviness of all of the guilt, shame, pity, and brokenness that comes with all we may have gone through and choose God's grace. Like 1 Peter 5:7 (NLT) says, "Give all your worries and cares to God, for he cares about you." I am human. You are human. We are human. As humans, we are going to experience some rough things in life and we are going to do some things that may not be the best. In fact, we may very well do what society deems the worst. But isn't it so great to know that there is a loving God who knows that you're human because He created you that way, but is also willing to take on every worry and every concern you have about your past in order for you to move on in the purpose He's crafted for you? It's like a magnet on a tray of nails. The nails create more weight on the tray, but as soon as you glide a powerful magnet over it, I assure you all of those nails become drawn up in an instant. God is attracted to getting rid of the things in our lives that hold us back because it creates situations where He has to prove He is God. From this moment on, let God show you that not only is He good, but He is God by allowing Him to carry your weight so that you may be free to share your story.

CHAPTER 5

THE TESTIMONY EQUATION

Now that we've addressed that, back to this equation I mentioned. Well, I guess technically in the math world, these would be considered proofs since it involves writing explanations of reason. The core of this proof is ultimately God's grace. However, it is our humanity that starts the proof off. It looks something like this:

Humanity → Testimony → Purpose = Proof of God's grace

Now with proofs, you tend to have to break down things with the definition of the concepts that make up the proof, so I'm going to do just that with help from the Merriam-Webster dictionary, starting with humanity:

Humanity – the quality or state of being human

Human – a bipedal primate mammal (Homo sapiens); a person

Testimony – a solemn declaration usually made orally by a witness under oath in response to interrogation by a lawyer or authorized public official; a public profession of religious experience

It should be noted that the reason I included the first definition of "testimony" is because it reminded me of something my dad said when it comes to us living our lives as believers for the world to see. He said if Jesus were on trial for being the Son of God, you sharing your testimony should be the thing to prove that He is indeed the Son of God. I paraphrased of course, but the gist of him sharing that was to keep at the forefront of our minds that, like the title of the previous section you just read, our testimony isn't just for us. It is to be shared with others for His glory.

Purpose – something set up as an object or end to be attained; intention

And lastly,

Grace – unmerited divine assistance given to humans for their regeneration or sanctification; a virtue coming from God

Conclusion: Your humanity, the state of just being a person and all of the things that come with that, is needed for your given account as to who God is through the evidence provided by Him in your life (your testimony). Your testimony is then divinely linked to your purpose, the thing God has specifically set up for your life for you to attain, and your purpose proves God's grace, His unmerited virtue on your life causing you to be set apart from the rest of the world.

Of course, I'm more of an English/Language Arts kind of gal, so there were more words than symbols or abbreviations used to draw out this proof, but when God gave this Heavenly download to me (as I like to call it), it was something that I just had to hold on to, something I needed to share. It gave me hope in the sense that everything God is doing, everything that we do, all of these pieces of our lives are all a part of one big thing that essentially points back to God's love and Who He is. God says in 2 Corinthians 12:9 (NLT), "My grace is all you need. My power works best in weakness." We don't have to create a façade of who we are when going to God. He sees us in our weakness, in our trials, temptations, pain, and heaviness, and reminds us that that's when He works best. Through God's love, and the choice of salvation, grace is attainable for everyone who chooses to believe in Him, and that He has a set purpose for your life that involves you sharing your story.

PART TWO

ACKNOWLEDING THE GRACELESS

CHAPTER 6

WHO ARE "THE GRACELESS?"

Now the moment we've all been waiting for. I know some of you may have had the question from the very start. You might've even been hesitant in picking up my book, nervous my theology may have been off. No worries though, I'm here to set the record straight. Who are the graceless? I know it might seem contradicting. "Essence, why in the world is this chapter, ***this book***, referring to 'the graceless' when you literally just said that everyone is capable of attaining grace?" Well, I'm glad you asked. I also mentioned that there are several other definitions of grace, so bear with me. After God gave me the vision to write this book, I knew there was going to be one word that stuck out to me the most; nope, not "grace"– "millennials." Now, when you think of the millennial generation what is the first thing you think of? Influencer bios on Instagram? Avocado toast? The diamond industry going out of business (or any other preposterous article title you may have seen floating across the internet or your tv screen)? Whatever it is, very rarely does the noun "millennial" have positive connotation. In fact, we're constantly deemed entitled or lazy, making it seem as if we are a nuisance to society, therefore, lacking grace. This grace I speak of is that of poise, elegance and sophistication; the grace that makes others believe you have your life together. However, because of the aforementioned concept of grace, we now know that whether some of these stereotypes be true and we do like avocado toast (*raises hand*) or do a pretty great job of being influencers on social media, that does not hinder our access to the gift that is grace. We still fit in the category of being saved by grace—it's that simple! So in this book, specifically this chapter, I want to bring encouragement from the ashes of ridicule that have been scattered by the negative stereotypes of society and those generations before us. I know I'm not the only one who feels this way, but sometimes, it's as if we've been deemed the generation that messed everything up for ourselves and instead of being poured into and mentored by those who came before us, it was easier for them to sit back, call us names, and watch us struggle to walk in our purpose. Father, forgive them, for they know not what they do. But Father, please also forgive us for allowing the things others say and do deter us from or make us hesitant in taking the path you've set before us.

Speaking of paths, let's take a quick trip to the book of Exodus. Most people know this as the book of Moses because it is here that we see the adventures God took Moses through to free the Hebrew people, God's chosen. However, I'd be remiss to assume that everyone knows the story of Moses, so I'll just give you the cheat sheet version! As a baby, Moses (after miraculously being placed in a basket floating down the river avoiding the jaws of crocodiles and tangles of exotic plants, according to the animated *The Prince of Egypt* film) was adopted and raised in Egyptian royalty, but he was actually a Hebrew. During this time, the Hebrews were enslaved, so when he grew up and it was revealed he, himself, was a Hebrew, it caused some confusion and guilt on his part that would later result in the death of an Egyptian at his hands and him exiling himself to the land of Midian. Fast forward a chapter, God calls him out via a burning bush and gives him direct orders to tell Pharaoh to "let His people go (iconic, I know)" and lead them into a new, fertile land, just for them, known as the Promise Land. Ultimately, the people of God were free, after a whole bunch of chaos and nonsense involving locusts, boils, blood, and so much more occurred, which resulted in them traveling in pursuit of the Promise Land. However, Moses and his generation did not get to the Promise Land. In fact, it took them 40 years just to get *near* the Promise Land. During their time traveling through the wilderness, their indecisiveness, lack of patience, and willingness to trust in God caused the Hebrews to delay their arrival to their promise. Needless to say, they were making the biggest, yet most wrong impression on the most impactful of people traveling with them – their children, including a man by the name of Joshua. Now, let's fast forward to the book of Joshua. After only getting near the Promise Land, Joshua and his generation picked up the slack of their parents and moved forward toward the Promise Land. Y'all…it only took them a matter of *days*! So what am I trying to say? Joshua and his generation were the ones who decided to do things differently to attain their goal of promise. That was the reason why they were able to access the land much quicker than their parents were – well, the reason they were able to access it at all. Joshua's generation chose not to take God's grace for granted and used the gifts embedded in them and the skills they had been taught, along with their full faith and trust in the Lord to accomplish something that had never been done before. There's a saying, "You are a product of your environment," which I fully believe to be true, but I also believe that as a product of a certain environment, you can either learn what to do or what not to do. Even as I'm sitting here jotting notes down for this book, a conversation is taking place about how "young people don't know how to build credit, write checks," etc. I could very well choose to respond in defense for myself and fellow millennials, but what I'm learning is sometimes, your defense isn't required, your example is. After being delivered from the hand of Pharaoh, promised a land flowing with milk and honey, and being constantly reminded that they were God's chosen people, Moses and his generation still chose a life of stubbornness and ignorance. From complaining about missing the food they ate when they were enslaved in Egypt, to building a golden calf to worship, they were wild! So God pretty much told them to keep that same energy and prevented them from reaching their promise. Joshua knew better. In fact, he got a front row seat to every performance of mutiny because he was Moses' assistant, thus, learning firsthand what to do and what not to do. After Moses' death, Joshua became the leader of God's people; he basically went from having an internship as an assistant to being the CEO. But it was in this new position that he flourished.

When looking at his journey throughout the book of Joshua, Joshua relied so heavily on the instruction from God in his life that he was favored greatly, specifically in the battle of Jericho. He was given clear, yet unusual instruction from God, including the direct order to march around the walls of the city in order to take control of it. His men could have told him he was crazy and chose not to heed to instruction because of how crazy it sounded, but I'd like to think because they saw what their parents did to Moses when He received instruction from God, they knew that probably wasn't their best option. As seen in chapter 6, Joshua and the people of God would go on to follow the Divine instruction of marching around the wall, with the Ark of the Covenant leading, for six days and then blowing trumpets and shouting the walls down on the seventh. Despite the illogicality in the instruction, Joshua abided in the promise of God, activated his faith, and positioned himself to execute and be the leader God called him to be. This would go on to be a faithful pattern of his throughout the whole book of Joshua, all the way up to the very end. But it is at the end where Joshua takes the time, before passing away, to encourage the people of God in their obedience to His calling and share with them the goodness and grace he, along with all of them, had been shown by God throughout their years. Joshua 24 is a full account of everything God did for them as a people and the testimony of Joshua as a leader.

I believe now is the time for us to be Joshuas; Joshua 2.0s, if you will. Choosing to boldly live for God with radical, unwavering faith is one thing, but then choosing to actually reflect on all that God has brought you through and encourage someone else through it, is another. We are the generation to do things differently. I know earlier in the book, I mentioned how it seemed like testimony service was only for old church mothers who broke out into impromptu hymns and spirituals. Well, now is the time for us to take our place and testify to the goodness of God in our lives, and the grace He has shown us, to encourage others throughout the world to get to know Who He is for themselves. Not because they were forced to by their culture's religion, not because their parents said they had to, but because He is good, His mercy endures forever, and He is literally the most abundant source of hope our world could ever need and receive. So, to the graceless, the Joshua 2.0s, I present to you the stories of those just like you and those nothing like you, the stories that may bring about questions but will hopefully also bring clarity and understanding, the stories that may make you laugh in rejoicing, but may also make you cry in relatability, the stories that will make you believe that there is a God who loves you, cares for you, shows His abundant grace differently to everyone who encounters Him, and wants so desperately to bless you with it so that you too may have an encounter as well.

***

"Ever since I was a baby, I'd always been reminded of how smart and gifted I was. From a very young age, I knew I was different. At the age of two, I began going to school and by the time I turned five, I was headed for first grade. My love for school and learning landed me in some pretty unusual cases that made me stick out throughout the years, including being the only one from my Kindergarten class to graduate, wearing uniforms every day to school when no one else was, and meetings with my parents, principals, and administrators determining whether it would be smart for me to skip certain grades. One year, my parents decided it would be best for me to transfer from the private academy I had known pretty much my whole life, to a school on a military base – basically the equivalent of a public school. I fought against it because private school education was what I had known my whole life. That, on top of seeing how public schools were portrayed on TV and movies: bigger classes, school bells because you were responsible for getting to class on time, and of course, scary social settings. It was all compiled into a big avalanche of fear. I worried about mean girls, bullies, different cliques full of popular kids, jocks, "nerds," all of these different people I would have to face. I was a little nervous— I was actually very nervous. While experiencing my own emotions, though, I didn't realize my parents were going through their *own behind the scenes. My mom was the current principal at my private school at the time, so when she announced the fact that I would be leaving, she was met with discourse from individuals that were a part of the school's faculty. She was pretty much told that I wouldn't survive high school because of the outcast status I carried with me, and because I was this anomaly, education was something I could achieve, but being accepted socially, I would never be able to grasp; not only in high school, but in college as well. Now I understand that these words weren't said directly to me, but they still impacted me heavily because when I did find out, it made my heart ache for my parents to have someone say this about their child. Also, finding out not only what the person said, but who the person was that said it – it can be a lot on you. However, I ended up flourishing in high school! I took Honors and AP classes, travelled Europe for athletics and extracurricular organizations I was a part of. I was selected as an All-American for academics and athletics, became the highest-ranking member of our JROTC Battalion in my sophomore year, and made plenty of friends and acquaintances all from different backgrounds. It was NOTHING like I saw on the TV screen. Of course, it came with its own sets of challenges; mean girls still exist, and people may always remember you as a "Jesus freak," but the very thing I was scared of, entering a new territory, I flourished in! In the end, not only did I "survive" high school, I graduated with honors earlier than I should have, and I went on to do the same thing for college (once again, college had its own sets of challenges too, but I survived and made a difference). And I know it's all because of the grace of God, because my parents kept believing in me, because of the standard of excellence I had for myself and most importantly, I'll say it again, God's grace. The unfavorable destiny someone spoke on my life was literally rebuked, crumbled up, shred to pieces, and thrown right back down to the pit of hell because God's grace showed me I was covered. The Word of God my parents spoke over me proved that my future was (and is still) going to be bright because of the plans the Lord has for me that will not harm me, that will allow me to prosper, and that will give me a hope and a future according to Jeremiah 29:11. So I share this to say no matter what someone may speak over you, remember what The One Who speaks TRUTH says about you. You were created for a purpose and you have a destiny! Don't ever let someone make you believe God's grace isn't true because of the way they see you. After all, Jesus took a pretty good number of outcasts and performed miraculous works with them."*

Signed, The Outcast That Overcame

"I was her. The woman who tried to be the glue. The one who fought endlessly for a man who wasn't meant for me. With hope awakened from my little girl dreams, in my eyes, he was everything. His approach was genuine with words like my father's. I fell in love. Nothing sexual, God-driven, authentic pursuit after Him, morning texts, daily prayers, the desire to grow together. The beauty of what we shared – time. Five months of many turns in the road, some joyous, most unpleasant. Withdrawn, anxiety-driven, what happened? Hurtful decisions, apologies given – forgiveness. New page. Moving forward, restoration, more dreams shared. Same page, one vision, only to discover he wasn't there. Critical opinions, mental abuse, lack of consistency, what more can I do? I love you. My desire is to keep growing with you. I love you. "Me too." The cycle continued and more hurt than love poured in. Red flags were present, but I wanted to keep trying again. I ignored the convictions God raised in my heart because I believed this was something He wouldn't allow to fall apart. When the worst of the worst settled in, the very thing I feared began: a new normal. The idea of parting from the one you love is a day you never want to accept, but when God has your heart, you learn to lean into the grace to be redefined again in Him. By His grace I live restored and renewed in vision. He has reminded me over and over of my wholeness

in Him. Never will he give us less than what we pray. His plans are to exceed our dreams in brilliant ways, only by His grace."

Signed, The Woman Who Overcame Shame and Leaned into His Grace

"The summer of 2014 I decided to work at a camp about one and a half hours from where I lived. It was a nice camp with friendly staff members, a list of activities to choose from, and a whole bunch of kids who looked up to you. It was great! As I was returning to my room at the end of one, long work day, I was looking forward to relaxing and putting my feet up for a bit before having to move on to our night activities. That is until I pulled out my phone and heard a voice message. We weren't allowed to have our phones on us while we worked due to the number of kids we were responsible for keeping an eye on, so this was my first time checking my phone after leaving for work. As I listened to the message, my heart sank to my stomach and panic took over; my friend wanted to end her own life. She felt hopeless and that her life had no meaning. She was ready to end her suffering from the life she lived. The first words I muttered as my fingers frantically dialed her number were, "Oh no you're not!" I was determined not to lose my friend and to speak to the greatness that was inside of her (and still is). As I heard the phone ring, I began praying over and over again for her to pick up. When she finally did, the sound of her voice shattered my heart. You could tell she truly felt lost and purposeless. So I began reminding her of her dreams, her goals, her passions, and why it was vital that she stayed here on this earth to fulfill those things. I then reminded her of our friendship, how long we'd known each other, the things she helped me get through, how much I loved her, and more importantly, how much God loved her. This is where I felt my faith was tested. You see, out of all the years we had known each other, my friend had always been very vocal about her disbelief in God. There were times where I'd bring Him up in *conversation and she'd make remarks, something along the lines of "I'm going to let you finish because I love you, not because I believe or agree." Though words like those cut deep, it wasn't because I took it personal, but because I knew if she would just surrender herself to God, it's not that she wouldn't go through the problems she was facing, but she'd know that The One who fights her battles for her and cares for her more than anyone in the world would be protecting her and loving her through them. I wanted her to experience just how great God's love is, but I knew I couldn't force her to love God either. As I sat there on the phone, the only answer I could think of was God. My First Lady recently asked the women in our church, "When was the last time you prayed a God hold-the-rain-and-set-the-sun-still prayer?" referring to a story we'd discussed about a woman fervently praying for God to come through on her request to prevent a thunderstorm from taking place during a moment of revival. Basically, a prayer that reminded God not only of Who He is, but of the power He says those who believe in Him hold. Well, this was that moment for me. I took one, deep breath and let out a trembling voice saying, "I know you may not want to hear this, but God is the only answer I can give you right now." I waited for a backbiting response or underhanded comment, but instead, I got a long sigh and an "I don't know." For the first time, I felt like she had repositioned her belief, or potential of belief at least. Though it wasn't an excited "okay!" it was a willingness to admit that it wasn't that she didn't want to have faith, she just wasn't sure of it. She became open. This was the first time she truly began opening up to me about why her disbelief in God came at such a full force. Her past experiences caused her to be angry with God and believe that He didn't care for her. At this moment, my roommate (we'll call her Jen) Jen walked in and recognized exactly what was happening just from my responses on the phone and began to pray out loud, withholding nothing. As I encouraged my friend on the other side of the phone and listened to her pour her heart out, I too was praying for something to take place – for her hope to be restored, a miracle to happen. But I was also asking the Lord to lead me and guide me on how to be the friend He needed me to be to her so she could truly feel loved. I stayed on the phone with her, listening and encouraging her all the way up until time for our staff's night activities. I asked her if she was going to be okay, and she assured me she was (I even snuck away and called to check in on her later that night just to make sure). I wanted to share this particular testimony because I think a lot of people are under the assumption that when situations involving unbelievers happen, the first thing, we, as believers, are supposed to do is try to convert them. But the Bible says that it is by grace, through faith, that we have been saved (Ephesians 2:8 NIV), so rather than going in with the sole mission to "save them," we must encourage and uplift them by showing them the love of God and speaking on the grace He has shown us that makes us believe, believing that God will do the rest. The latter part of that scripture says that being saved by grace through faith is a gift from God, and it truly is a gift worth sharing. The way I see it, sometimes, people may not like the gifts you choose to gift them with, but you never know what their response will be until you present it to them. She didn't get saved or confess her belief in God that night, but I am a firm believer that even in the midst of her disbelief, He still calmed her storm. Both Jen and I knew what the power of prayer was and continues to be; the ability to speak to our Heavenly Father directly, to make our petitions known and for Him to hear our heart's deepest desires without interference. His Word also states that when two or three are gathered, He is in our midst, He is there with us (Matthew 18:20 CEV) and that's exactly what happened that night in our little camp cabin. Oh, and Jen (you know who you are), if you ever get to read this, I just want you to know that I am tremendously thankful for you and your willingness to set aside your own plans in that very moment, drop everything and begin praying on behalf of someone you didn't even know. You are the epitome of a prayer warrior, and I'm so honored to have accessed the throne of grace with a sister-in-Christ like you! I love you!*

Signed, The Believer Believing for A Friend

"Imagine being the parent of a child you were told by several doctors wouldn't be able to play, walk, or run. That was the reality for my parents. This journey started for me at the age of three. Technically, it started at birth, but my parents didn't find out until I was three. During a normal (or I guess what they thought was going to be a normal) checkup one day, doctors discovered something wrong with my back and when they looked in my records, they saw I had been diagnosed with spina bifida upon being born, yet my parents were never told. With the way things were looking with my spine, plus the rate I was growing, doctors were quick to say I'd have difficulties for the rest of my life. I am truly blessed, however, because I was raised by two strong believers. As soon as they received this news, they instantly went straight to God. My dad even reminded God constantly, over and over again about what His Word said regarding healing and that because He is God, He has to abide by His Word. My parents then enlisted prayer warriors from all over the world to join them in prayer, praying for my complete healing and my future. At the age of four, I was told I had to get a CT Scan and an MRI done in order to see the progression of everything that was happening in my spine. I remember being in a hospital gown that was too big for me, nervously approaching this big machine, just to find out I had to get in that machine and lay in it. I put on a brave face for my parents as they comforted me and assured me that everything was going to be okay. No four-year old should have to experience something like this, but it had to be done. As I got in the machine, I was instructed to lay "very very still." Though there was the buzzing of the machine and the other electronics that supported it, all I remember was the stillness I felt.

Nervous, scared, but courageous. My dad then grabbed hold of my foot sticking out of the machine and began praying for me and crying out to God in the most fervent, yet quiet way. Instantly, I felt peace, so much so that I fell asleep and still don't really know how long I was in there for. When we got the results back, they found traces of scoliosis. But we kept praying. I tested again weeks later, and when we got the results this time....nothing was found! This was a testimony that would forever change my parents and our household. I went on to be a varsity soccer goalkeeper, averaging 13 saves a game, and becoming an All-American in Athletics and Academics. You can't tell me God's not good!"

Signed, God's Favorite Goalie

PART THREE

MY FIRST DATE WITH GRACE

CHAPTER 7

THE GRACIOUS RENDEZVOUS

I've never been on a date before, so the first date experience still awaits me. However, there have been a couple of first date stories I've heard that reminded me of the first time I vividly remember encountering God's grace, especially those good first date stories you hear about. Words like nervous, excited, awkward, and perfect have all been described for feelings of that one first date; you know the one that led to you falling in love, marrying your best friend, and finding your life-long adventure buddy (evidence I've found from others who've shared their experience). That's how I would describe the one, sticks-out-in-my-head encounter I had with God. When my eyes awakened, and I knew I had a real relationship with Him – my first date with grace. I felt like this chapter would be the perfect opportunity to not only share my own "first date" story, but those of my friends that have gone to experience even more encounters with God, but still remember that "one." I presume these stories will be reflective of what real, good first dates are like – varying, but perfect in their own way. Prayerfully, these stories inspire you to look forward to having your own rendezvous with grace today.

***

"Math is my least favorite subject of all time. If it hasn't been mentioned or emphasized in this book enough already, now you know. However, there were two particular topics in math that I found in high school that really piqued my interest, one of them being Geometry. I had a really, really, really great Geometry teacher; however, she was not the nicest teacher, so you had to make sure you were always on your "Ps" and "Qs," that your "Ts" were crossed and your "Is" dotted. If you didn't, she would call you out, and it wasn't to make us feel bad. She just wanted to challenge us and make sure that we stayed aware and paid attention in class, that way, we could be receiving the best education possible. Well, one day after lunch, because I always had this class after lunch, and you know that after eating you get tired – you catch the "itis" as some people call it – I went to class and I was just gone, like, I was exhausted. I was just sitting there and I couldn't even hear what she was saying; it was like a muffled voice almost because I was just in my thoughts thinking, "Oh my goodness, I'm so tired. I'm so exhausted and she's going to call me out, and I'm not going to be able to pay attention. I'm not going to be able to learn this new concept…" and just going on and on and on. So then, I started praying like, "Lord, I need you to do something," and it's funny because later on in life, it was situations like this and a few others that caused me to develop the phrase "Jesus, be an energy drink (because He can be anything we need Him to be, so why not ask Him to be our energy?!)!" So in **that moment, I was like,** *"God I really, really need you to do something to wake me up because I can't afford to make a bad grade in this class or to be called out by her." I kid you not, it was like as soon as I prayed that prayer, my teacher called on me and I instantly received a jolt of energy. It was as if I had just*

downed two shots of espresso in 5 seconds. She proceeds to call on me and asks, "What's the answer?" My thoughts then begin to scramble in my head as I internally freaked out. "Oh my gosh! God I wasn't paying attention! What's the answer?" Sure enough, I looked down and the answer was right in front of me. I told her the answer and she says, "Correct! See, she was paying attention." I just thought it was the funniest thing, but also the scariest because I literally prayed specific, back-to-back prayers and they were answered completely. That's when I realized even in the stuff that seems so small, God wants to be involved in it. He wants me to know that He cares for me, He doesn't want to see me fail, and there's nothing too small for Him to do! I know we tend to focus on nothing being too big for God, but there's nothing too small for Him either. That's the great thing about grace; it comes in all forms, shapes, sizes and packages. You can never get too much of it, you can never get too little of it. As I said before in this book, there's no such thing as miniscule grace. Grace is grace. So that pretty much sums up the first time I truly realized the value of my relationship with God – well, that I even had a real relationship with God – and experienced my first date with grace. As I look back now, there are many other times I can point out in different stages of my life where grace has been applied, but this was my first encounter, my first date that I could truly remember experiencing grace for myself."

Signed, The Girl with Geometric Grace

"I think one of the testimonies that I would use is probably how God has shown Himself to me, where I can be confident in who I am in Him, and because of that, I do not have to fear people or situations – which I'm still working on it, but I've come a long way – where it's hard to say 'no' to people or it's hard to stand up for yourself because of fear of men. God showed me 'why fear man? What can he do to you?' Also, when it comes to feeling like you need to 'pay back' somebody, God says that, 'vengeance

is mine' (Deuteronomy 32:35 ESV). *You give everything to God when you're alone, when you're scared, fearful; you give everything to Him. Being alone, you wind up going into these 'I'm trying to find something to satisfy me' moods, instead of relying on God. Or 'if they don't think I'm important, then I'm not important.' So for me, that often went into seeking other people's approval and how they feel about me and what they say, then it turned into 'if I can get a guy's attention, then that shows I'm pretty good about myself. I can handle my own.' Now instead of seeking friendship, I find myself putting my worth in a guy's hand instead of God's. Here I am – I want peace, I want somebody to tell me that I'm worth it, but I'm not going to God Who says that I am. Maybe because I couldn't really see Him or hear Him. Or maybe I wasn't trying to listen. But now that led to lust. In order to 'keep' a guy, you gotta flirt with them, so now I'm flirting, they're way ahead of their time, and I'm over here trying to be somebody I'm not. They're teaching me things that I don't even know, but here I am going with the flow to get a guy's attention. So now the lust led to pornography, and the pornography led to trying to go out and find somebody that can give me that satisfaction that pornography did. I felt like 'well, if I see it, and it looks good and makes me feel good, then maybe I should go and try it.' All of it was just fake, anyway, but I didn't know that. I was just trying to grab onto something instead of holding onto God. That definitely took a while to let go of. There was kind of like a David moment where somebody came to me and told me 'hey, this is what you did.' And it's like 'oh wow,' I didn't even realize, because I'm so caught up in myself, that I hurt God and the people that care for me and are around me. I believe that goes into grace because I didn't really understand God's mercy until I felt like I really, really needed it and felt like I wasn't worthy of it. You know you can tell other people, "Hey, God forgives you, God loves you," and not truly grasp it yourself until you have to receive that same forgiveness. It was really hard for me to accept that. Then, I was told that even in my self-pity, shame and guilt, I can idolize and put myself first. I was holding onto lust, but now I'm holding onto shame, guilt, self-pity, and 'woe is me' instead of letting that go and just going to God and saying to myself, 'Hey, He loves you.' So it did take a long time – the healing process took a while. I do believe that I did not hear from God during that season because it was all me. But when I heard Him again, and I felt His grace and His love, it was a relief, but at the same time it was also heavy. I guess that's what was meant in the scripture that talks about about how '[His] burden is light' (Matthew 11:30 NIV). It was a little bit of a burden to realize that no matter what I'd done and will do, He still loves me and forgives me. My mind couldn't really accept that. I'm just like 'what?!' But I also don't want to get to that point again, where I'm also like David, up in the rooftop just chillin' when I know there's a battle I need to get to (referring to the story of David in 2 Samuel 11). But just knowing that God's grace is there for me through my ups and my downs, it definitely helps me get through the next thing."*

Signed, Self-Confident in Him, Not Men

"*In high school, I remember my dad took me to a church where he was a guest. They had my dad sit up front, so we were separated. They had a guest prophet who was just flowing in the prophetic, talking to people, and when he started laying hands on people, miracles started happening. I moved up to the front where my dad was, and as he (the guest prophet) began talking to another lady who had come up, he looks real quick over at me, like dead at me. My heart dropped. I looked at him thinking, "Oh, what is he about to say?" He went back to speaking to the lady, and then in the middle of ministering to this lady, he turned back to me, completely stopped everything he was doing and everything he was saying, and began prophesying to me, telling me how God was going to use me. So I think, "Okay cool." Then he turns to walk away, and while he was doing that, I had a really fast thought in my head. I don't know why, but I thought, 'What about my husband?' I had that thought in my head so* quick, and as soon as I thought it, he turned around and said, 'Don't you worry about your husband!' I said, 'This dude legit read my mind, he read my mind!' He said, 'Don't you worry about your husband. God, right now, is your husband.' At that age, I wanted to be married early; it was one of my greatest desires. At that moment, though, it switched my focus. That was nothing but the grace of God. First of all, I was in awe of the power of God operating through that man like that and how God used him, because he had no idea who I was and I had no idea who he was. To this day, it's one of the top memories in my head of when I first was like, 'Oh my goodness, God is real!' It also brought to my consciousness that there's so much more to God than what I originally knew, and it made me feel like I have to figure out who God is. That was the thing that ignited something on the inside of me to chase after God, figure out who He is, and live the way that He wants me to live. When I made dumb decisions with people I dated, every single time, God would always speak to me and I would run back to God. That was my very first encounter with the grace of God to where I was like, 'Yo, God is real and He loves me and cares about me. He doesn't want me to make any stupid decisions. He wants me to do right.' That was the first wake-up call for me and ever since then, every single time I've heard God speak, it was so easy to be like, 'Yes, Lord.'"

Signed, Wowed by His Wonders and Amazed by His Grace

PART FOUR

THE STRUGGLE IS REAL, BUT SO ARE WE

CHAPTER 8

USE YOUR VOICE

Just a heads up, this may very well be the longest chapter in this book, so grab your pen, paper, and popcorn because we've got some things to discuss. Some may question why I'm as passionate as I am for our generation. If Chapter 2 isn't any indication, I'll make it simple for you: we have a voice! We have things to say, stories to share, perspectives to offer, and are yet constantly being turned away. I believe it is my job not only as a believer, but as a millennial to encourage young people like me, even those who aren't in my generation, but especially those who are, to know that we have purpose! I know that our decisions are constantly questioned, our views constantly challenged. But those things have only been presented to us as weights, not to carry, but to make us stronger in what we believe so that we may be ready to speak when given the platform and assigned the time. And y'all, trust me; I know the opposition is real. I literally just experienced it a few hours ago.

I was invited to a function for singles. I figured would be a nice little event to attend. Unfortunately, I was only one of three people in attendance to fit in the millennial demographic. But I wasn't going to let that stop me from trying my best to have a good time, even if that did mean sucking on butterscotch candies and conversing with people almost three times older than me. As the night went along, names were called, prizes were won, and the place was alive and well. While crossing the room to get to my purse, I was stopped by the commentary of an elder woman. "You know young lady, back in my day, we wouldn't purposely buy jeans like that with holes in them. If our jeans had holes in them we'd toss them out," she said in a rather priggish tone. What she didn't know was that this wasn't my first rode-- err — exchange regarding my wardrobe choices, specifically my "holey" ones. Rather than heading for retreat, I turned around and politely countered with "That's funny, I was actually just having this conversation." I then proceeded to tell her about how my generation, being different, learned to embrace what used to be deemed impoverished and used it to create style. "Rather than having to throw out clothes due to economic status, we kept them and made it fashion." Well, my opposer was soon joined by a sidekick who, after repeating nearly everything she already said, chimed in, "You need some patches, young lady." It was almost as if the phrase "young lady" was used to be interchanged with an insult or a hit taken to my intellect, but that could just be me. I didn't let the comments stop me, though. I went on to speak to the elderly man, the sidekick who recommended patches, choosing to provide further understanding into the reasoning behind the fashion choices of the millennial generation. The topic this time: cropped pants and men's suits, you know, the ones that show the ankle. I explained how "high waters" were such a common theme for young growing boys, that rather than having to constantly spend money to buy slacks that would temporarily fit, ankle-length trousers became the fashion. His response? "Well, you'll know it's fashion when me, your dad, and pastor show up to church wearing them. That's how you'll know it's fashion!" I could tell he was getting a little worked up over our discussion, so in an effort to lighten the mood, I responded, "Actually sir, that's when we'll know it's out of fashion," with a little giggle. Instead of the light chuckle I hoped for, I was met with more sarcastic opposition. "And when we show up with long earrings dangling from our ears and tattoos all over us, that's when you'll know it's fashion. But we won't because it's not fashion!" It was at that moment I knew the best option was to let this rushing train run off its tracks until it lost its momentum and stopped when it was ready. He was now going on a tangent about a woman he saw with kids who, according to him, "looked like they hadn't been fed well in two years." He proceeded to describe the woman, noting the multiple tattoos that covered her body. This erupted into him questioning and assuming the choices of the woman and whether the cost of her tattoos could've been what has prevented her children from being "fed well." By this time, he had captured the attention of almost everyone in the room and concluded with a daring declaration while looking me straight in my eye. "But that's *your* generation." My heart sank. My eyes sort of stung as if tears wanted to fall out, but they never did. He just proved the very reason why I was writing this book. I wanted to respond with something, but it was as if my lips were literally glued shut. As my friend, the third millennial in attendance (the second was the daughter of another lady at the event), entered the room, I met her with grateful eyes of desperation. "Thank you so much for coming back." She had gone to move her car while all of this was taking place. "Oh no, what happened?" she asked. As I caught her up on everything she missed, she began to encourage me in knowing that not only did I maintain respect in the way I spoke, but I was speaking to them out of a place of love and an attempt at providing further understanding. We left shortly thereafter, still smiling, and thanking the host. As I got home, my friend sent me a quick text to check up on me. where I merrily replied that at least that night's events would make a great 1,000 words somewhere in my book, and as you can see, here they are!

On a serious note, I think my emotional response stemmed from the fact that part of me didn't want to believe this was actually happening, that this was our new normal; having to constantly defend our decisions about what we wear, why we're on our phones, what genre of music we listen to, just to prove that we're still worthy of being seen. We're still worthy of being heard. Don't get me wrong, I understand how all of these things and the way we use them (the way we dress, the activity we involve ourselves in on social media, the artists we choose to listen to, etc.) can greatly affect our character as Christians. Romans 14 does a great job of making it clear that everyone in this life has a customized character and way of living, but if your plan is to make them feel accepted and welcomed into the body of Christ, you are not to belittle, shame, and "quarrel over opinions" with the person who is looking for that refuge in God. This is where things get tricky for us. You see, because millennials and younger generations are identified by the very things that are so easy to pass judgement on (fashion, music, technology, etc.), we become the breeding ground of opinionated remarks and relentless ridicule disguised as blankets of concern and care. This is the new normal. It sucks, but it's true. But that doesn't mean we stop being who we are and who we've been created to be. We keep going.

I feel like anyone who has ever been a teacher of some sort can relate to what I'm about to say, so let me make sure I say this clearly. Teachers may give out tests, but we (and I can't stress this enough) get tested every single day! Talk about staying on your toes, and quick-thinking on the spot; in order to survive, we make it happen. One strategy I had to come up with for my three, four, and five-year olds involved snuffing out those who really needed to go to the bathroom, and those who just wanted to get up and play because they were bored. Needless to say, this was most effective at naptime because going to the restroom was a class activity rather than an individual one due to lack of supervision from a teacher while the class is sleeping. So I came up with a strategy and it went a little something like this: the student would raise their hand, and after calling on them, would tell me they needed to use the bathroom. An observant teacher knows all of the background info and cues for each student regarding their scheduled activities, especially when it's time for them to use the restroom. So after telling me they need to use the restroom, I do a quick rundown of all activity that took place before the child asked, who the child is, what their background is, and determine my answer from there. I'm going somewhere with this, I promise. I usually met their question with a question of my own, "It's almost time to wake up. Can you hold it?" Not to make them potentially pee on themselves (sorry if that's TMI), but because I knew that the response I'd get back would be the defining moment of truth. For some, they'd simply respond with a "yes," go back to sleep, wake up from the nap, then be so excited about snack time they forgot they asked me about the bathroom in the first place. But then I had my other ones, the ones who were desperate. They'd tell me they have to go, I'd ask if they could hold it, and they'd respond "yes," but then they wouldn't go back to sleep. They'd wait for about two minutes, raise their hand again, and tell me they'd have to go again. This is when I knew they were serious and would find another teacher to help supervise. Well, at least that's what my four and five-year olds would do. My three-year-olds, on the other hand, would just keep telling me over and over and over until I'd find someone to watch my class so I could hurry and take them. (newly potty-trained kiddos with patience isn't really an expectation one should have in the classroom). My point in all of this "potty talk" is that if you have something to say and want your concern to be known, you don't choose to go back to sleep and forget it ever happened, you keep talking until a change is made. I've said it before, and I'll say it again: We are the generation that does things differently. This means the change we want to bring about will have to be brought about – you guessed it— differently. But how will others hear our voices if we're the ones who choose to silence ourselves? I don't think my lips were glued that night at the singles event because I didn't have anything to say. In fact, on the contrary. Maybe God glued my lips shut because He knew that everything I wanted to say, everything I wanted to pour out from the deepest depths of my heart: the desires I have for this world, the hopes I have in my generation, all of it could not be expressed or understood in a way they (the older people at the event) would be willing to receive. I could've cried my eyes out while telling the stories of people I know who were ignored and given up on, and in turn, gave up on themselves, ending up in situations no one deserves to be in. I could have pulled up photos on Facebook of what former friends looked like before and after the ungodly influences they succumbed to. I could have even shared my own stories of what the words of others had previously caused me to think about myself, and the way I saw myself that took years of undoing. Or I could have gone straight home, grabbed some ice cream, and blast "Nothing Nice to Say" by Mogli the Iceburg, to get my mind off of things. But instead, I chose God's grace. I chose to use that time to reflect on the things God has brought me through, the things He protected me from, who He says I am, and more importantly, what He has called me to do, in ripped jeans or not. The words I've written on these last few pages could not have been used in that moment to bring understanding. I know this now because they were reserved for you, in this moment, to be written at 7:19pm on a Sunday, so that as you read them or hear them, you too, would be encouraged to keep speaking so someone can hear your heart – hear your voice. And sometimes, your voice may not be verbalized over a PA speaker of some sort. In fact, more often than not, your voice is captured through your gifts, the unique abilities God has graced us with to purposely help someone else. At that event, while being chewed out over a pair of distressed jeans (and possibly a top showing my shoulders, not certain, but wouldn't be surprised), I wanted so badly for my voice to be heard by those who were choosing not to listen. I could have easily decided to internalize what I was feeling, hold it all in, but I choose to keep talking. I choose to let my voice be heard and not stop myself from sharing my experiences. It doesn't matter how crazy, mundane, or "basic" they may seem because I know that ultimately, the more I keep talking, the more I keep choosing to operate in the gifts God has given me, the more likely it is for someone to hear me and for things to change.

CHAPTER 9

WRAPPED A LITTLE DIFFERENTLY

By the time you've reached this point of the book, there are two big things you already know about me: 1. I'm a teacher and 2. Say it with me now… I can't stand math. While these are pretty important things for you to know, if we're going to be friends, hopefully they're not the only thing you take from this book. I have to admit, though, teaching has provided me with some pretty great insight and revelation regarding what has, is, and will be discussed in this book, so I just stick with it. That was a segue.

I'd like to think that one universal lesson most teachers teach is to "be the change," usually with some assistance from Mahatma Gandhi. I mean just think about it; ever since we were kids, starting from preschool or even daycare, how many times have we heard about being the change, making a difference, being the difference, making a change, and any other interchangeable phrase that points to ultimately doing something to change our world? There's a reason for that. It's because it's expected of us! It's expected of us to be these young innovators and engineers, politicians, doctors, lawyers, and creatives. The problem most tend to run into, though, is not that we aren't striving to get to these things, or that we don't have the desire to want to be these things. In fact, we are these things…we're just not what people expected. This is funny, considering these great expectations placed on us, huh? It's kind of like this: almost everyone loves Christmas, especially little kids. The one thing that tends to attract them the most is the idea of receiving presents. Imagine being a fly on the wall of a family who has a small child, and that child specifically asked for a doll. If the doll was wrapped in festive gift wrap, with shiny details and a pretty bow on top, the child would probably be so ecstatic and ready to open it that they'd get straight to ripping off the paper. The same with a gift bag. It may not have a big bow on it, but the appearance is enough to make them excited about throwing tissue paper onto the floor just to get to whatever the gift is inside. Now imagine the child receiving that same gift, the very gift they asked for, but it's wrapped in some plastic cling wrap, aluminum foil and fabric. The child may be hesitant in wanting to open it because it doesn't look like any of the other gifts that they've seen before. However, the gift remains the same, it's just covered in a different wrapping method. That's what's happening in our world. Our gifts are valuable and we're learning how to go about using them in a way to make a difference in the world, but we're just not wrapped in the way people expect us to be. But guess what? That's perfectly okay. 1 Timothy 4:12 (my favorite Bible verse of all time) in the New Living Translation says, *"Don't let anyone think less of you because you are young. Be an example to all believers in what you say, in the way you live, in your love, your faith, and your purity."* So rather than accepting the stigmas and stereotypes placed on us, we've literally been instructed by God, through His guidance, to go and prove to others, through our actions, what we say, think, speak, and do, that we are here to serve God the way HE wants us to. We are commanded to exemplify our love, faith and purity so that when others see these things in our lives, they know without hesitation that we belong to God and that we've been called to be what our teachers have desired for us for years – world changers.

CHAPTER 10

BE THE DEMO

I remember when I was little, there was a time where kids meals from fast food places came with CD-ROMS with games on them (shout out to all of the people who know what I'm talking about). I had this one particular BMX game that was my favorite, but before I could get good at it (and I was very good at it), I remember having to watch the demo. During the demo, I was shown what keys to use, what their functions were, what my objective was, and pretty much everything that would help me be successful in playing the game. If I hadn't been shown the demo, I may have figured out how to play the game, but it probably would have taken me a while to fully experience the game and know all of the options I had and prizes I could win. That's kind of how I see the younger generation. If you're like me, you might have a quick moment of thought where you think something along the lines of, "Well, that's not fair. The older generations are the ones who are supposed to be showing us how to do things in this life. They're supposed to be our example." But isn't it amazing that when looking at the scripture aforementioned, 1 Timothy 4:12 (NLT), it's directed at us as young people to be the example? Y'all, we have to be the demo! Whether it be for the older generations or the newer generations, we must be the ones ready to go out into the world, bearing fruit – using the fruit of the Spirit to cultivate opportunities of ministry, shining our light, and willingly dedicating our lives to living for Christ, and Christ alone. And it all starts with your testimony. Oh, and before anyone reading my book from an older generation may think I'm bashing them, firstly, thank you so much for reading, but secondly, I assure you that's not my intention at all! The point I'm trying to get across is that you, too, are the younger generation to someone else, just as we as millennials are currently the older generation to generation Z, generation Z is the older generation to the generation after that, and so on and so forth. It's a generational system that's been set in motion ever since the Bible days. What I will say, though, is that if you found you were able to see some truth in any of the things I shared regarding the societal perception of the older generations, now would be a good time for you to denounce those things and choose to embrace the change taking place from God through this new generation of believers He's raising up. It may be hard to trust someone who's still learning about who they are and why they've been placed on this earth, but remember, that was once you too. I know many of my elders talk about passing the baton or passing the torch, but you can be more than just the baton-passer. Be our cheerleaders, our coaches, our running buddies through this course of life. That way, after passing the baton, you'll never really stop running the race, you've just become a part of the support system for someone who is. Pass the torch in full confidence, knowing that you spoke life and encouragement into a generation that is trailblazing like never before. Going back to addressing my generation: stay the course with your purpose. And if you just so happen to see someone from another generation cheering or running alongside you, be sure to let them know how much you appreciate and cherish them.

Hopefully, this is the last time I mention it, but I am not a fan of math. I just think it's so funny (and the reason why I keep mentioning it) how sometimes God uses the very thing we cannot stand to help us make sense of things. For example, when writing this book, I was given two equations involving the believer, grace, and purpose. I discussed the first one a little bit earlier in my first chapter, The Concept of Grace. Well, like most mathematical elements, here is an equation to add onto the other equation (proof) that I discussed earlier. I call it "The Associative Purpose Property." The associative property of an equation, from my understanding, says that no matter how you decide to group or re-group numbers in an equation, the answer will always remain the same. This is kind of how I view purpose. As believers, we are constantly told that the joint purpose of The Body is to "go ye therefore, and teach all nations, baptizing them in the name of the Father, and of the Son, and of the Holy Ghost," like Matthew 28:19 (KJV) says. But in that objective, many fail to realize that we've each been given a tailor-made blueprint to follow to fulfill that instruction to where, ultimately, no matter how we do what it is God has called us to do, the command of Matthew 28:19 should be met by each believer. "Go ye therefore" is not just an encouragement, but a direct assignment to the fulfillment of your purpose on this earth. Your purpose requires your testimony, as discussed in the proof in Chapter 1.

However, you may not realize that your joy is connected to your purpose, which can be ironic, considering it's our testimonies, the stories of how we overcame the hard things in life that are also needed for our purpose. The things that bring you bliss despite the circumstances you may face or the state that our world is in – these things play a vital role in the discovery of your purpose. So where does your joy lie? Is it in helping others through volunteer work? Is it in using various forms of art to showcase the expression of your passions? It could even be simply making people laugh! Wherever your joy stems from, there your purpose is cultivated. Now I already told you the thing about grace, so here's the thing about joy. Joy is so powerful that it washes over any impact the hurt within your testimony could have caused. It's not to say that what happened didn't impact you in a mighty way, but it is to say that the hope found in joy cannot only make you see why you had to go through what you had to go through, but be grateful for going through it too.

***

"When they finally gave me my epidural, the doctors kept saying his heart rate was dropping. They kept trying to flip me, get him to wake up, and get his heart rate back up. After his heart rate dropped so many times, they told me, "If it drops one more time, were going to take you in to have a C-section." Of course, I didn't want a C-section at all, so I started believing God and praying. One of the nurses came in saying, "Well, when you go in for your C-section..." talking as if they had already made the decision that I was going to get a C-section and I looked at her in her face and said, "Y'all don't have to tell me about no C-section because I'm not going to get a C-section. I'm not." I legit cut her off while she was talking. You could hear his heart rate on the monitor, so I could hear when it was dropping. When I heard it start to drop, I laid my hand on my stomach and God spoke to me and told me to pray over him. So every single time it started to drop, I laid my

hands on my stomach, decreeing and declaring that his heart rate would come back up. And I'd speak to him and tell him, 'No, no, no Micah. Bring your heart rate back up." Each and every time I did that – I was in labor for 14 hours – multiple times, I did that, his heart rate came up every single time. Before the nurses could come in, before they could say anything about it, his heart rate would come right back up. When I gave birth to him, he was healthy, he was good. But a couple of days after I gave birth, he ended up in the NICU because of his blood sugar. Each time his blood sugar needed to be taken, it was so nerve-wrecking because they would say, "If his blood sugar is not up by this time, then he's going to have to go into the NICU. I was freaking out instead of praying, and he did end up in the NICU. So in order for him to be out of the NICU in the time I wanted him out, he had to have good blood tests from then on out. They hooked him up to IVs. I sat there and cried watching him get stuck with a whole bunch of needles; it was horrible. They said I could stay in the NICU as long as I wanted or that I could go back to my room, so all throughout the night I would go to the NICU and feed him. After I'd feed him, they would take the blood tests and I heard the Holy Spirit say every single time I fed him, to pray over him; every time I did skin-to-skin I prayed over him and commanded his blood sugar to come up. The hospital wanted to send us home without him, so I was rushing to have him out of the NICU. Every single time they took his blood sugar, it was where it needed to be at. They had to take it every two hours on the dot. If he passed six of them, then they would spread out the time to see how much longer he could go with keeping up his blood sugar. When everything came back good, they took him off of the solution they were providing for him to see if he could hold his blood sugar on his own. I would continue to pray over him, just like I was doing before whenever I fed him and whenever I did skin-to-skin. By the end of the next day, his blood sugar ended up being fine and he came back to our room, out of the NICU and his blood sugar has been perfectly fine ever since. Through this,

God helped me increase my faith, commanded me to speak, and pray instead of freaking out. That's also where God showed me His grace and being there for me and instructing me, but out of my obedience He moved for me. Now, I have a healthy little boy. He has no issues, no problems, and is growing just fine.

Signed, The Millennial Mama Covered by Grace

PART FIVE

IF HIS GRACE IS LIKE AN OCEAN, ARE WE SWIMMING?

CHAPTER 11

TEXAS AND TUBIN'

Living in Texas, I quickly learned that floating the river is just as much a community sport as attending a Friday night lights football game. The Comal River is an iconic Texas River that flows through the town of New Braunfels. One afternoon, my friends and I decided to go hang out at Comal River at this picnic space called Landa Park. I'm not a swimmer (and hopefully, by the time this book is released, I will have finally started learning how to swim), but I do enjoy the presence of water. I tend to correlate it with peace and serenity, even if I am just looking from afar. As I was observing the activity going around, I noticed people in line to slide down the water slide and swing off the dangling rope above the river. I noticed little ones with their parents and grandparents strutting down the water pathway with inflatable floaties on each arm. I noticed kids play-fighting with pool noodles and lifeguards telling them to be careful. People-watching with my feet in the river just seemed so nice and relaxing; I was content. My friends, however, were swimming and chilling in the actual river. I watched as the coolness of the water automatically soothed them from the scorching heat that I was still experiencing despite having my feet in the water. I was hot, but I still feel content. As time went on, I watched as one of my friends gave another friend an impromptu swim lesson. As their arms motioned and feet fluttered, I couldn't help but begin to wish that I was involved too. And it was almost as if my friend heard my thoughts because she then shouted out from the river "Essence I know you don't know how to swim, but are you sure you don't want to get in? The water feels really nice!" After turning her down a few times I finally admitted that it wasn't the lack of swimming lessons that were keeping me from getting in, but the fact that I wasn't wearing a swimsuit. A few things came to me in a revelation during and after this event, one of them involving a song.

"How He Loves" by John Mark McMillan was the inspiration for this particular chapter. When I first heard it, I instantly fell in love with it. The funny thing is, I'm pretty sure the first time I heard it was at the same youth camp that made me question whether or not I had a testimony (I could be wrong, but I really do think so). There just so happens to be a particular lyric in there (I won't quote for copyright reasons) that compares God's gift of grace to us to a body of water that everyone has access to and is submerged under. Whenever I listen to it, I picture a blue abyss of water with gentle waves moving throughout. However, I'll be completely honest, it was always hard to imagine being submerged. Submersion, being engulfed, is usually connotated with something negative, especially when dealing with people; unless we think of water baptism. But I feel that if you are like me, your first thought may be that of drowning rather than getting baptized in your church's baptismal pool. It makes it seem as if there's no way of escape, and maybe that's what John Mark McMillan's perspective was. Maybe he wanted to convey that He sees God's grace as something that not only overwhelms us, but surrounds us in such a way that we can't escape unless we, like those who usually find themselves sinking in water, try to fight against it. But allow me to offer yet another perspective. This in no way negates the perspective of others, just something that was revealed to me in hopes of understanding my relationship with God and His grace even more, and that I'm hoping may inspire and encourage you too.

CHAPTER 12

FLOATING. SINKING. SWIMMING

When I think of swimming, three particular actions come to mind: floating, sinking, and actually swimming. One we're told to enjoy, one we're cautioned against, and the other is expected of us. But when it comes to grace, especially in the context of grace being an ocean, which action do we commit to? Fair warning: this may get deep… pun intended.

Floating: the most relaxing of the three options; the most comfortable. With floating, you create your own environment of comfort simply by choosing to stay above the surface, not being submerged. However, this can easily be interrupted by the motion of those around you who find themselves swimming, enjoying the water in their own way. Water splashing on you, the yells of one swimmer to another, usually leads to a response of some sort.; whether it be irritation and frustration brought by the disturbance of your comfortability, or FOMO, the fear of missing out, because you realize that the true action begins *in* the water.

Sinking: the most dangerous of the three... physically. I understand when most people compare to sinking in something, they may be thinking of it from the perspective of allowing yourself to be fully covered and engulfed by something. However, from an emotional and/or spiritual perspective, I feel like that sometimes it is in our engulfment that causes us to become paralyzed by or stagnant in something. We become so overwhelmed resulting in limited motion. Though grace is one of the best things to be overwhelmed with, I believe it is a gift that shouldn't just be kept to ourselves because while we're drowning in the grace that God has blessed us with, there is someone above surface just floating in the comfort of their sin because they feel they aren't worthy of truly experiencing God's grace.

Swimming: ah, yes. The most action-packed option. Swimming, in reality, is used as a form of exercise, something to get you from one place to another, and an activity shared amongst other fellow swimmers. Though floating is also another activity that can be mutually shared, it is with swimming that you are able to create more opportunities for fellowship with those around you. For example, that day in Landa Park, if my friends and I all had tubes and were just floating on the river, it would be a nice experience, but with swimming, as shared previously, my friends were able to have swimming lessons, talk, laugh, and have a good time while experiencing the refreshment of being in the water. I, too, would have joined them, but felt I couldn't because I didn't have a swimsuit. I'm here to tell you don't be like me.

Don't let the excuse of not having a swimsuit keep you from experiencing the enjoyment of swimming. Spiritually speaking, of course. I don't want you to assume I'm saying you don't need proper swim attire to go to your community pool. What I mean is, a lot of times, people feel that before they can come to Christ, they have to "get ready first." We, as believers, have probably heard multiple times, "Come as you are," but for some, they really don't believe that they can. They put an expectation on what encountering God looks like, starting off with a presentation of who you are outwardly and inwardly. And if you've realized "they" is actually you, here's some encouragement for you. God already knows the inner and outer parts of you and guess what? He loves you anyway. He wants to be able to show you what He can do in your life, for you and through you! Don't hold yourself back because you feel like you don't look the part. Jump into His grace! Experience His refreshing presence and love in your life. If you don't know how to swim, I promise you He will bring someone along your way to give you swimming lessons, and before you know it, you'll be swimming right alongside them, helping others learn to swim and experience the ocean that is God's grace.

If you are reading this book, and after coming all this way through multiple pages, reading and receiving whatever messages may have pricked your heart, you realize you need to give your life to God or simply step back into the grace and love He once showed you before you decided to walk away, this section is specifically for you. The Bible tells us that because we are believers, we will purposely endure hard things. But in you, making this decision right now to choose to be washed clean and link up to God, you're declaring that no matter what life presents you with, you will choose to embrace God's grace and the purpose He has given you through your testimony, no matter what. Like David, you are crying out *"Create in me a clean heart, O God. Renew a loyal spirit within me."* (Psalms 51:10 NLT)

The Word of God says in Romans 10:9 (NLT) that *"If you openly declare that Jesus is Lord and believe in your heart that God raised him from the dead, you will be saved."* Our salvation takes two things that stem from one: Choice – our decision as to what it is we will do. Salvation requires our choice to use our voice to declare who Jesus is and that He's in control of our lives, and the choice to believe that very statement with every inch of our being. God is a God of love. He will not force you to do anything that you do not want to do, yet again, showering us with His grace through the gift of choice. So today, I pray for you, my dear friend, that the Lord will speak to you right now and show up in your life like never before, showing you that when you choose Him, it is **always** the right choice. But not only do I choose to pray for you, I choose to pray with you. Right here and now. So if you'd like, please join me in approaching the throne of grace:

Father God,

Thank you so so so much for your love and kindness, Lord. Thank you for being who you are: the King of Glory, the Lord God strong and mighty in battle, the One who chases our hearts down time and time again just to prove how much you care for us. God, your Word says that you delight yourself in the details of our lives (Psalm 37:23 NLT); you care about literally every part there is to us and what we experience in life, God. So help me Lord, help us, to hold onto your love and hold onto your grace no matter what situations we may go through in this life. God it is through your love and mercy we have access to grace in the first place, so help us to be mindful of the favor you desire to give us. Help us to have the mindset of your Son, Jesus, when He was crucified. It was because of the joy He knew He had awaiting Him that He endured the cross for our sake (Hebrews 12:2 NLT). So it is for the joy set before us of pleasing you, living the life of purpose you want us to live, and the joy of bringing others to know who you are through our shared stories, our testimonies, that we choose to endure what we go through. We believe, God, that you sent your Son to die for our sins and the sins of every person in this cruel and dying world. God, we choose this day to confess with our mouths that Jesus is Lord and you have complete rule and reign over our lives. We don't want the pressure of having to live this life by ourselves, Lord, so take control of everything here and now. Sometimes, life can seem so hopeless, Lord, but it is with you we receive peace that surpasses all understanding (Philippians 4:7 ESV) and an abundance of hope! We choose, this day, to believe that you raised Jesus from the grave, three days later, signifying your Truth, your Word, and your promises that never fail, creating the Gospel of salvation that brings hope. We choose right now, from this day forward, to bask in your love, swim in your grace, and tell others about how wonderful you are, through the power you've given us in the word of our testimonies.

We ask and pray all of these things in Jesus' name,

Amen.

***

"I feel like this testimony is so significant to me because it's one of the things that made me truly realize I have purpose, a huge, fantastic, God-given purpose on this Earth, and I'm here ready to do what it takes to live it out. When my mom was around my age, she was diagnosed with an autoimmune disease known as lupus. There were doctors that counted her out from the very beginning, only giving her very few months to live. Technically, this is a testimony within a testimony because she literally just celebrated her 50th birthday and is such an amazing woman of God, it's not even funny. But back to my part in this: my mom was given a short time to live, but she and my dad chose

not to give into what the doctors were saying. After a couple of years of being together, my parents were ready to start a family. Well, because of this disease, she was told she wouldn't be able to get pregnant, but if she did, she probably wouldn't be able to carry it to term. As soon as my parents heard this news, they began to pray. They got their church family involved and soon everyone in agreement was not only praying for the healing of my mother, but for a healthy pregnancy to take place. Fast forward to my mom being pregnant. My mom was not only pregnant, she was pregnant with twins! I'd imagine the excitement was high amongst their friends and family, knowing that God moved on their behalf. However, for my parents, that excitement was soon replaced with sadness. One day, while at the hospital, my mom found out she had miscarried. My twin had passed away. The doctors were now telling my mom that in order for her to have her best chance of survival, I would need to be aborted. Wow, I think this is the first time it's really hitting me. I can't even imagine having to experience what my parents had to in that moment, what my mom had to go through. How do you go from one minute being told that you have this disease that's more than likely going to take your life before you can see your next birthday to being told that now in order to live, you'd need to get rid of your baby right after losing your other baby? The faith you'd have to have in knowing that God is real and still true to His Word despite enduring all of that is astounding. But that's my mom. Her faith was, and is still to this day, unshakeable. She chose to continue with her pregnancy, carrying me to term. During that time in the womb, I was literally fighting for my life while my mom fought for hers. Naysayers doubts went to battle with the prayers and decrees of the righteous. A spiritual battle with words and the spirits they carried, and the Angels of the Lord's Army was taking place on our behalf. Whew, God is so GOOD!!! Like so many people would've given up! My mom could have given up on me. She could have given up on God. But she chose not to. She trusted Him, *reminding Him of Who He is and all He's done in her life, that this would be no different. He would deliver on His promise because He loved her, because He loved my father...because He loved me. After the tears, after the pain, after the heartache, but more importantly, after the prayers that were cried out desperately to the Lord over and over again, I was born on a Tuesday, February 20th, 1996. My parents named me Essence Amouré meaning "the abundance of love (being that we lived in Europe, they were inspired to make a European fusion for the spelling of my middle name); a reminder of who God is and a declaration of who I am meant to be in this world. The time that it took me to write this book will forever be cherished because so much was revealed to me, including just how powerful and astounding God's grace is. Not just in seasons of hardship, but in our day-to-day lives. My mom chose to worship God and give Him glory despite her sadness, despite her pain. How much more can I worship Him, knowing that I was a result of His promise to her? As I write the last few pages of this book, I lay here mesmerized at how good God's been to me. The moments I've taken for granted have now been shown to me as replays for spotting moments of His grace, and when I tell you His mercies are new every day, I mean every day! But through this testimony, through this book, I've seen not only His grace in my past, but the grace He's given to me in my present for my future! Thank you, Jesus! To think that I am such a valued piece of God's plan for revival in this world that He'd give me life, literally, to accomplish my purpose for His glory. That's why I share my stories. That's why I try my best to speak to the greatness in people. There's so much more to why we're here than just to be here. We're not just here to exist. There is a calling so strong on our lives that our God will literally do the impossible, the unthinkable just to make it happen because he loves us. So to whoever reads this book, or even chooses to just glance at this page, know that you have purpose. You are not an accident. You were purposely created by God to fulfill the destiny he has set on your life. My pastor, Pastor*

Bill Coker, in a message once said, "Live in purpose on purpose," and that has been something that's stuck with me ever since. God makes no mistakes, so it's time for you to value the life He has given you by knowing that you are to be used in the best ways for your joy and for His glory. His grace is sufficient, it's enough, and you have the ability to experience it every day by choosing to embrace purpose. I do not take this life for granted and I'm thankful beyond measure. So until the day He chooses to come back, I vow to flourish in purpose, tell my story, and live abundantly in His grace."

Signed, Essence Patterson, Author, Millennial, and Citizen of Grace

ACKNOWLEDGEMENTS

Firstly, I'd like to thank my Mommy. Your life is literally "Goodness Grace Us" personified. Without your constant love and support, I don't know where I would be. Thank you for always pointing me back to God when things seem to get tough in my life. Thank you for speaking greatness over me before I even entered the world and for continuing to do it every chance you get. Your love for me has been revealed in such varying ways, but the instant support you gave when I shared you with my "writer's secret" is one of the most profound things that will forever stand out to me. Thank you for being the moon, teaching me to shine through the darkness. I love you forever and always.

To my Daddy, I hope I made you proud! I know you tell me often that I do, I just never want that to be something I take for granted. Thank you for all of the conversations we had leading up to this book, during the writing process, and the ones we'll continue to have because of it. The excitement and zeal you have for conversing about God and how awesome He is, is something I've picked up and hope to never let go of. I may not have ended up at UNC or be that fitness instructor you'd hoped I become, but I thank you for the constant support you've shown in each stage of me trying to figure out my life and its purpose. Thank you for believing in the hope of my generation and thank you for believing in me.

To my book mentor, Kyle, hearing your testimony from the get-go generated an automatic "yes" for me when it came to who I needed to surround myself with to make this vision God gave me a reality. Your work is not in vain, and you more than anyone, know just how valuable your purpose is. Continue to use your shining light for His glory because it is most definitely bright!

To my accountability partners, Stef, Becka, and Fe, I love y'all so much! Not once did you complain about me texting at weird hours and your instant "yes" to my ask warmed my heart more than you know. Your support is forever appreciated. I can't wait to see what comes next!

To my fellow FAM leaders, Stevie and D, can y'all believe something we talked about briefly one night after Bible Study turned into this?! I'm so grateful to be in ministry with you all. Thank you for your constant encouragement and steadfast assurance of "we got your back." I look forward to more grace-filled adventures with you guys!

To Pastor Coker, you may not remember it, sir, but you spoke this very thing into being. I know that that was the working of the Holy Spirit, but ever since our families were introduced, you've been praying for me. That's over seven years' worth of prayer, something not to be taken lightly. I appreciate you sir – your love and light in ministry is commendable. Thank you for covering me.

To my editor, Faith, I appreciate you tremendously. It's one thing for me to be an English lover, but having to juggle what I wanted to share, with authenticity, while being sure I conveyed my message in a grammatically correct way, was a burden you lifted off me. Thank you, thank you, thank you!

To my Launch Team members, you all make me so happy! Knowing the amount of love and support I had backing this book was one of the biggest motivations I had for finishing the last leg of the race toward completing it. But I want to specifically thank you for choosing to be my cheerleaders and coaches as I run this race in life. Your encouragement and willingness to serve is inspirational. I love you all!

To my confirmation callers, Jesse and Ms. Diana, thank you for calling me. You choosing to simply pick up the phone and check up on me was one of the greatest things that could have ever happened. You two were the final signs God gave me in knowing that I had been released to write this book. Thank you for your obedience in following His voice and thank you for the instant encouragement you gave when I picked up. I can't wait to see how God is going to move in each of your lives.

To my babies, my angels, thank you for teaching me! Thank you for showing me daily what unconditional love looks like. I miss you so much already, but I know you're going to be the best group of Kindergartners Texas has ever seen. I pray my generation does well in setting a Godly example before you so that when it comes your time to run, you'll know without a shadow of a doubt that we're rooting for you and not against you. Te amo, I love you forever and ever (in German and sign language too)! P.S. Cleo says hi!

To my anonymous contributors, thank you for being so open and willing to share your stories not only with me, but with the world. It can take a lot to let down your walls and allow someone to see what kind of hard things you had to go through, but when God is in the mix, it becomes one of the best things we could ever do, and I think each and every one of you know that. I'm grateful to God for blessing you with new life and new perspective after trusting Him in your hardships and I pray that He continues to give you fresh vision and a renewed sense of purpose as you go out into the world to continue sharing your story. I love you all so much!

To Andy Mineo, KB, Social Club Misfits, and Trip Lee, thank y'all for creating the soundtrack to writing this book. Knowing some of your testimonies sparked even more fervency in wanting to convey this message of grace to our generation. Thank you for using your gifts to bring God glory and creating something I can Milly Rock for Jesus to.

To Jonathan McReynolds, thank you for your obedience to God in using your gifts. Your music got me through many, many, many hard seasons in my life, and I'm so thankful to serve a God who uses a guy who performs in socks and always beats the Cracker Barrel peg game to help in my breakthrough. God first revealed that my humanity is necessary for my testimony through you. So, thank you for being human, but more importantly, thank you for sharing your gifts with the world while being human.

To Pastor Michael Todd, first off, you're awesome! I don't think that it's ironic that y'all released The Marked Series around the time writing this book became prevalent in my life. Your impact on our generation is monumental and I'm so grateful to live in the same era as you to see what God is going to do with our generation. Thank you for speaking life and hope into us. Thank you for seeing the creativity and greatness God has embedded in us not only individually, but as a whole force. We're literally a unit of world changers, and we get to have the honor of having you as one of our leaders in battle. Continue to serve the Lord with all your heart, sir. I can't wait to see what He's going to do next!

ABOUT THE AUTHOR

Essence Patterson is a former proofreader, Editor-in-Chief, and PR Coordinator turned writer. Raised in Europe, but a resident of Texas, she graduated from Texas State University where she received a degree in Public Administration and Mass Communication. In her spare time, she enjoys laughing with her mom, dad, and little brother, Christian, researching the origin of idioms, and creating vision boards on Pinterest while listening to the 116 Clique. She is also an alumna of Enactus, an international business organization that encouraged her direction in public speaking. Being the millennial expert she is, Essence loves having the ability to speak to and on behalf of her generation on various platforms, and is now using the pen God has placed in her hand to do just that.

To keep up with all of Essence Patterson's activity follow her social media links and visit her website:

www.essencepatterson.com

Instagram: @essence_patterson

Facebook: facebook.com/pattersonessence

Made in the USA
Lexington, KY
22 July 2019